Performance Measurement System for the Public Works Manager

Utilizing the Compstat and Citistat system within Public Works

Sergio P. Panunzio

authorHOUSE®

AuthorHouse™
1663 Liberty Drive
Bloomington, IN 47403
www.authorhouse.com
Phone: 1-800-839-8640

First published by AuthorHouse 8/5/2009

ISBN: 978-1-4389-6474-4 (e)
ISBN: 978-1-4389-6473-7 (sc)

Printed in the United States of America
Bloomington, Indiana

This book is printed on acid-free paper.

This book is dedicated to
Angelina and Paolo,
I love you both immensely.

Contents

Chapter One The Basics

Chapter Two Building a Team

Chapter Three Tasks

Chapter Four Going Live

Acknowledgments:

To say that this book was written by Sergio Panunzio is an understatement. All of my acquired knowledge is merely a summary of my experiences and difficulties I have encountered throughout my career.

Throughout the research for this project, I have thought fondly of friends, colleagues, and directors that I have had the fortune to both work with, and learn from.

I can never forget the support that **Bruce D. Walter**, from Union City, provided as my career was starting. I will never forget **John Kennedy**, a superb business administrator, who inspired me. In addition, the "Positive re-enforcement, and hours of therapy" that I have received from **Ron Manzella** and **Frank Bradley** gave me the impetus to put this idea into print. I also have to thank my friends, **Henry, Joe, Pat, Connie, Steve, Luis, Onix, Vinnie, Jesus , Scott, Mike, Kelly, Jaci,** and **George** for your time and patience with me.

During my most difficult times, I was always supported by my dear friends, **Tina, Charlie, Giulio, Giovanna, Tomas,** and **Paolo**. Thank you for the love, comfort, and support you provided me.

Preface

As I complete this book and read it over again, I cannot help to think what it would take for the Public Works industry to get the recognition that it deserves. As I write the final chapter, my television shows President Obama stating that "The solution to the crisis is a large stimulus plan through Public Works".

Isn't it amazing that for the past three decades, and especially after 9-11, the Public Works industry has taken a back seat in the chain of *"Respect and funding"* within our government agencies but as soon as the economy bottoms out, the only way to solve and rescue America from this problem is through Public Works!

This manuscript is designed to provide the Public Works Manager the tools to compete with Police, Fire, Health and Senior Services for funding so that our industry will receive the recognition it so deserves.

Performance Measurement System for the Public Works Manager

Chapter One

THE BASICS

Our daily services are all too invisible
to the naked eye until things go awry.
We must do a better job to communicate
the value of our services.

W hat is performance management?

To some people, performance management means collecting performance information. To others it implies an appraisal. Utilizing the Compstat and Citistat system within Public Works book's definition incorporates a range of different tools and activities used to drive improvement.

I define performance management as: "Taking action to increase performance of services for users and the public ". Action may be at individual, team, service, organization or department level.

Improvement to outcomes should benefit service users but does not always mean increased service levels – sometimes better outcomes can mean delivering better value for money.

Reducing levels of service in one area may free up resources to be used more effectively elsewhere. Performance management will look different in different places, but effective organizations share some common characteristics.

These are:

+ Real-time, regular and robust performance data

+ Can-do culture inspired by strong leadership

+ Agreed lines of individual accountability

+ Clear performance management review, combining challenge and support

+ Transparent set of performance rewards and sanctions

Effective performance management requires:

+ Systematically deciding and communicating what needs to be done (aims, objectives, priorities and targets)

+ A plan for ensuring that it happens (improvement, action or service plans)

+ Means of assessing if this has been achieved (performance measures)

+ Information reaching the right people at the right time (performance reporting) so decisions are made and actions taken

These plans and actions fit within a framework that I summarize as 'plan, do, review, revise' later in chapter three "Tasks". Through this framework, learning can be harnessed in a continuous cycle of improvement.

All aspects of management overlap. For example, leadership is not in itself performance management but is essential to its effective use. To work well, it must be coordinated with other systems, such as financial management (directing resources to areas needing improvement or strategic priorities) and risk management (managing risks to avoid failure).

To begin, the entire concept of this program is to spread the message about the success and service provided by your Public Works Department. The responsibility of our department is to ensure that services are rendered efficiently and effectively.

We must continue to ask our resident what changes are needed. Our ultimate goal is making government work in this new information age.

In recent years local government projects have been handicapped by declining citizen confidence, and financial constraints. Basically, citizens do not feel that government understands their concerns, or that citizens have a significant influence on community and local financial decisions.

Most residents are acutely aware of government shortcomings, but far less willing to pay for unnecessary expenditures and are even less conscious of the benefits municipal government provide.

KEEPING UP WITH CHANGE

With the change of the dynamic of the uniformed departments and the quest for our industry to demand the respect that we deserve, a perfect storm was created.

The uniform divisions no longer have an advantage when attending budget work session. As our elected officials are aware, we should make it our point of advising, that we are now educated through an accredited university and state certification.

More importantly; our certification needs to be maintained by obtaining Continuing Education Units throughout a three year period. This certification is something that our counterparts in the uniform departments are not required to do.

We all look the same. No "Scrambled eggs" on our hats and no badges. Now Public Works managers and Police and Fire Superiors wear suits or suitable attire. We have successfully leveled the playing field. The national homeland security department also aided the bridging of these "Big three" with the inception and mandate to have all Public Works entities train in Incident Command, better known as NIMS.

Then why do we still have an identity complex?

How is Public Works going to compete with the existing uniform departments reporting methods?. Well, as my father often said "If you can't beat them…Join them!." That is exactly what I intend to do!.

Compstat

Compstat was the Police Department's best kept secret!

Compstat—or COMPSTAT—(short for COMPuter STATistics or COMParative STATistics) is the name given to the New York City Police Department's accountability system and has since been replicated in many other departments.

Compstat is a management philosophy or organizational management tool for police departments, roughly equivalent to Six Sigma or TQM, and **is not a computer system** or **software package.**

Instead, Compstat is a multilayered dynamic approach to crime reduction, quality of life improvement, and personnel and resource management.

Compstat employs geographic information systems and was intended to map crime and identify problems. Through weekly meetings, ranking NYPD executives meet with local precinct commanders from one of the eight patrol boroughs in New York City to discuss the problems.

They devise strategies and tactics to solve problems, reduce crime, and ultimately improve quality of life in their assigned area.

Compstat originated in the New York City Police Department in 1994, under leadership of Police Commissioner William Bratton and Deputy Commissioner Jack Maple.

They modified conventional community policing ideology after realizing that, to reduce crime and respond to communities' needs, many operational decisions should be made by commanders at the precinct level. They reasoned that precinct commanders are in a better position than headquarters executives to appreciate and meet their communities' needs, and so gave precinct commanders to give the authority to make the decisions and recommendations as needed.

They also determined that precinct commanders are more cognizant than patrol officers to understand and unify the agency's policies with the social dynamics of their geographic compass. To enact this change, Bratton revised

NYPD policies to empower precinct commanders, significantly expanding their authority, responsibility and discretion, as well as their degree of control over personnel and other resources.

As their authority was expanded, their responsibility, discretion and accountability increased as well. Bratton's ideas are based on community policing and the Broken Windows Theory by George L. Kelling.

The LAPD has further expanded Bratton and Maple's work and the results from New York into COMPSTAT Plus. The operations of COMPSTAT include weekly reports, accountability, profile reports, strategy meetings and technologies.

When Martin O'Malley took over as Baltimore's Mayor in December 1999, the city government suffered from rampant absenteeism. In the Department of Public Works, for example, one in seven employees failed to report to work every day on average. This absenteeism required other employees to pick up the slack, which produced high overtime costs and a huge burden on the city's finances.

O'Malley decided to tackle this problem by implementing a data-tracking and management tool similar to CompStat. This was the birth of CitiStat.

EXERCISE

Research for the budgetary appropriations of Fire, Police and Public Work under "Capital Improvements or bonding".

Make a comparison chart of the appropriations. Compare them and discuss .

CitiStat

CitiStat is a performance-based management group within the Baltimore's Mayor Office assigned with improving service delivery to the city of Baltimore. The Citistat system used the same tenets, process, reporting, and multilayered dynamic approach to quality of life improvement, the delivery of services and personnel and resource management as their predecessor Compstat.

CitiStat Tenets were developed from the tenets created by Jack Maple for New York City's Compstat – a strategy that uses timely and accurate crime data to inform policing efforts. CitiStat uses the same tenets to provide timely, reliable services to Baltimore's residents.

The tenets are as follows:

1) Accurate & timely intelligence shared by all

2) Rapid re-deployment of resources

3) Effective tactics and strategies

4) Relentless follow-up and assessment.

I will go into details of each tenet in a later chapter.

History:

Our industry has historically been the platform for certain employees to seek alternate employment (Usually to the uniform services), and to our fault, services have really never been reduced. When compared with uniform departments Public Works does not offer as many opportunities or advantages as the police or fire divisions.

Originally, the industry was driven by labor.

The earliest evidence of urban sanitation was seen in Harappa, Mohenjo-daro and the recently discovered Rakhigarhi of Indus Valley civilization.

This urban plan included the world's first urban sanitation systems. Within the city, individual homes or groups of homes obtained water from wells. From a room that appears to have been set aside for bathing, waste water was directed to covered drains, which lined the major streets. Houses opened only to inner courtyards and smaller lanes.

Roman cities and Roman villas had elements of sanitation systems, delivering water in the streets of towns such as Pompeii, which featured building stone and wooden drains to collect and remove wastewater from populated areas - see for instance the Cloaca Maxima into the River Tiber in Rome. But there is little record of other sanitation systems throughout Europe until the Middle Ages.

Unsanitary conditions and overcrowding were widespread throughout Europe and Asia during the Middle Ages, resulting periodically in cataclysmic pandemics such as the Plague of Justinian (541-42) and the Black Death (1347-1351), which killed tens of millions of people and radically altered societies.

Very high infant and child mortality prevailed in Europe throughout medieval times, due not only to deficiencies in sanitation but to insufficient food for a population which had expanded faster than agriculture. This was further complicated by frequent warfare and exploitation of civilians by brutal rulers. Life for the average person at this time was indeed 'nasty, brutish and short.

Here in the United States, Boston is credited in establishing the first sanitation department, mainly due to early English influence. Shortly thereafter, New Amsterdam (Now New York City) established public works sanitation department.

In recent years, the department of Public Works has become a broader term of its original inception. Originally, Public Works was described as internal improvements.

Internal improvements were defined as a constructed object that augments a nation's economic infrastructure; examples include airports, canals, dams, pipelines, tunnels, railroads, roads and artificial harbors.

Today, in many municipalities, the Department of Public Works is defined as a uniformed force of unionized sanitation workers. Their responsibilities include, but are not limited to, sanitation and recycling collection, street cleaning, snow removal, water treatment, wastewater treatment, road repair, shade tree maintenance, and public building maintenance.

This industry is one of the most advanced in local municipal government.

Years of neglect in the employment of prospective candidates has created a negative public image. Often the term "Politically connected" were hired, some of them with handicaps, but able to perform "**Labor**" work.

This worked for many years, while labor was the driving force of the industry. As technology advanced, Fire departments moved from the horse drawn water tank to mechanized engines with pumps. As with the Police Department, technology advanced, and quickly moved to modernized radio dispatch centers and alternative crime solving techniques. The Public Works department advanced as well, but not as rapidly as their uniformed counterparts.

This is not to say, that there have not been improvements in the industry. A more appropriate term may be a shortfall of "ground" to the uniform services.

As Police and Fire departments lobbied and increased their importance, and expenses, science and technology enabled them to become more efficient. As building and construction codes became more stringent, fires occurred less frequently, and the fire companies became less active.

Crime scene technology became more advanced, and technology allowed for cameras and global positioning systems in police units, making a police force leaner and more efficient.

Exercise

Research the history of the city or township that currently employs you. Specifically, research history of facts about the Fire, Police and DPW, throughout the town or city's history.

Compare and discuss.

In order to reduce costs, elected officials began to decrease the reliability on a Police or Fire Chief, and opted for more affordable options. The Public Safety Director. These events and other similar dynamics all came together in the late 80's. In 1980, the New Jersey Public Works community effectively lobbied the state legislative body of the state and a new legislation was introduced.

Credit is often given to Ray Manfra (retired) for effectively lobbying for the Certified Public Works Manager Law. Ray Manfra envisioned an opportunity to correct past imperfections. Almost as if being in the right place at the right time, Ray began to design a basic blueprint for every Public Works manager. The program is divided into nine course parts. There are three major sections: Management, Technical and Government.

Management

+ Management, Tasks, Responsibilities, and Practices
+ Managing and Developing Human Resources
+ Public Relations for Public Works

Technical

+ Operations Resource Management
+ Information and Records Management
+ Municipal Planning and Urban Development

Government

+ Local Government in New Jersey
+ Municipal Budget Process
+ Public Works Purchasing

To educate our public works administrators and give official recognition to the program, Ray sought help from an accredited institution. With the assistance of Rutgers University, a curriculum was installed, and legislation was introduced in the State Assembly. A certification program from an accredited and respected university was just what the industry needed. The New Jersey Certified Public Works Manager law enabled managers, superintendents, directors and other Public Works leaders to receive the training, education, and knowledge available previously only to the uniformed departments.

In effect, what the industry did was to send a clear message to our counterparts and elected officials that we were not going to accept their insinuations and we as a whole were willing to do whatever was necessary to make it stop. At first the program was expected to fail. How could the industry expect experienced men whom have been doing the work for years, to attend a classroom course?

Well, the trade impressed everyone by having numerous individuals go through a rather rigorous course. Many failed the state exam, retaken the test and passed. In the early 90's New Jersey became the first state in the union to have a Certified Public Works Manager program Public Law 1991c258. To this day, New Jersey is the only State of the Union that has such requirement for Public Works managers.

EXERCISE

Research and compare your municipality vs. surrounding municipalities, how many have a police/fire chief as compared to directors?

Is there an assumption amongst those municipalities to convert to a director?

Compare and discuss.

The Budget

Elected officials, like to decrease the bottom line, but not at the expense of reduction of service. The more they decrease the budget, the more they expect services to remain or in actually increase.

As managers became educated, the uniform departments lost their edge. Annually, each department must present a budget.

Budget refers to a list of all planned expenses and revenues. It is a plan for saving and spending. A budget is an important concept government. In other words, a budget is an organizational plan stated in monetary terms.

The purpose of budgeting is to provide a forecast of revenues and expenditures and how it enables the actual financial operation of the business to be measured against the forecast.

In today's government budget preparations are performed on a calendar or fiscal year basis. As more and more communities enter the technological world, the process if often televised or publicized. This allows for the elected officials to demonstrate their fiscal conservativeness and be dogmatic about their political position to the constituents.

These budget preparations are almost always proceeded by a memorandum or directive to department heads to "Reduce each line item" by a politically impressive number. This number (Usually a percentage) initially will be inflated then developed into a reasonable number, or rather *realistic* number.

This allows local elected officials to announce plausible deniability when taxes increase. The departments are especially impacted by these *"Cuts"*, because the managers' only true direct impact is on the *"Other expenses"* category. All municipal departments fight for every single budget dollar.

In short, the budget is divided into two basic parts: other expenses and contractual obligations. With contractual obligation, there is really no control of increases and decreases. The other expenses can be controlled by reducing the operating costs on a particular line item. In the past, at these public hearings, commonly known as budget workshops the Police and Fire Department had an advantage.

Describing these budget hearings, a colleague of mine once said that the Police and Fire departments had an upper hand because of "Uniform intimidation". As comical as this may sound, but true, he described one of many hearings he had attended in the past. He described the elected officials on the dais, well dressed with lots of books, manuals and other paper in front of them. A few, if any, concerned residents in the audience.

As the clerk of the board opened the meeting, the township administrator began speaking about the future forecast. He begins addressing the money management tactics of prudent investments for the community. At a specified time each department director is scheduled to be questioned, line by line about its requested appropriation.

The Police Chief is usually first, as the biggest department of the municipality. He usually attended the meeting, in full uniform, with badge, citations and *gun.*

He is flanked by the deputy police chief, who is wearing the identical items. The only difference between the two is that the deputy police chief has less *"Scrambled eggs"* on his uniform hat. They come with a statistician, usually a police superior with the responsibility to put together the presentation and collect numbers and data all year long.

The elected officials begin praising the Chief and his *"Men and Women"* for reducing crime and making the community safer. As elected officials enter the painstaking process of explaining line by line item, there is an exchange with the police, regarding ideas in reducing the amount of the police budget. The Police Chief turns to the Captain, whom opens a briefcase and takes out a book. The book is known as the **"Uniform Crime Statistics Report"** or UCR.

The Uniform Crime Reports (UCR) contains official data on crime that is reported to law enforcement agencies across the country that in turn provide the data to the Federal Bureau of Investigation (FBI). UCR focuses on index crimes, which include murder and non-negligent manslaughter, robbery, forcible rape, aggravated assault, burglary, larceny/theft, motor vehicle theft, and arson. UCR is a summary-based reporting system, with data aggregated to the city, county, state, and other geographic levels. Crime statistics are compiled from UCR data and published annually by the FBI in the Crime in the United States series.

The chief normally changes the direction of the meeting to the previously discussed reductions. He and his staff effectively point out that any reduction will decrease effectiveness of programs and increase crime. This is often supported by statistical trends, specific percentages and charts.

As elected officials hear this, a quick retreat is made of all previous statements and full budgetary appropriations are reinstituted. The Police chief leaves with an untouched budget, no increase, and high accolades from the elected officials and residents. He leaves.

Thereafter, the Fire Chief presents his budget. He is in full uniform, with badges and citations and a nice white hat with scrambled eggs. He is also flanked by a deputy chief and a fire officer.

Again the latter's job description is usually the training officer, and compiling statistics for reporting purposes. At the meeting, exchanges are almost identical as their police counterparts the elected officials on the dais insist on reductions in budget line items. As this discussion progresses, the fire officer opens his briefcase and hands the chief a book. The book is called the NFD Report.

The National Fire Data Report is a book, like the Police's UCR that is a collection of fire related data collected by the National Fire Center. The collection, analysis, publication, dissemination and marketing of information related to the nation's firefighting effectiveness is broken down into states, counties, and municipalities for their reporting purposes.

The Fire chief, who learned from his police counterpart, again effectively argues for reinstatements of funds on the line items. There is another presentation, supported by statistics, charts and percentages. Fire presentations that show "Feel Good" photos of a cat being rescued and children attending a fire house tour are much more effective than the police presentation. The elected officials are impressed and at the strike of the gavel, return all funding to the fire department. The last of the big three, as these departments are often called, is the Public Works' superintendent. As he enters the room, he is not flanked by anyone. He has a quasi-uniform, shirt but wearing jeans, often smells of cigarettes and his tie is undone.

Sensing he is uncomfortable, the dais begins firing questions and place emphasis on efficiency. In between there are a few compliments, but far and few. As he witnesses his budget being cleaned out, he has no data to rationalize his expenses, no fancy charts or percentages. Public Works departments do not have a UCR or an NFDR. This is about to change.

EXERCISE

Research and chart, statistics for the Fire, Police and Public Works, within your municipality, for the past three years.

Answer the following questions and present to class.

Are there any statistics, to compare year to year, of how many pot holes were repaired?

Are there any statistics, to compare year to year, of how many burglaries were recorded in town? How many fires? How many EMS Calls?

Are there any statistics, to compare year to year, of how many storm sewer drains were cleaned?

Culture

Your organizational culture was formed over years of interaction between the participants in the organization.

W e must first define what culture is before we can consider changing it.

The American Heritage Dictionary defines culture as, "The totality of socially transmitted behavior patterns, arts, beliefs, institutions, and all other products of human work and thought characteristic of a community or population." For our purposes we'll define culture as a pattern of beliefs and expectations shared by the organization members.

These beliefs and expectations produce norms that shape the behavior of both individuals and groups within an organization. Culture is usually long-term, strategic, and difficult to change. It is rooted in beliefs and values. In other words, culture is a concept that represents the shared sense of the way we do things. A critical factor in guiding day-to-day behavior in the field of organizational studies and management which describes the attitudes, experiences, beliefs and values of an organization. It has been defined as "the specific collection of values and norms that are shared by people and groups in an organization and that control the way they interact with each other and with stakeholders outside the organization."

This definition continues to explain organizational values also known as "beliefs and ideas about what kinds of goals members of an organization should pursue and ideas about the appropriate kinds of standards of behavior organizational members should use to achieve these goals. From organizational values develop organizational norms, guidelines, or expectations that prescribe appropriate kinds of behavior by employees in particular situations and control the behavior of organizational members towards one another."

EXERCISE

Can you identify within your department the different "Cultures" that exist?

Identify and defined them, prepare a presentation.

Organizational culture is not the same as corporate culture. It has wider and deeper concepts, something that an organization 'is' rather than what it 'has'. Senior management may try to determine a corporate culture. They may wish to impose corporate values and standards of behavior that specifically reflect the objectives of the organization. In addition, there will also be an existing internal culture within the workforce.

Work-groups within the organization have their own behavioral quirks and interactions which, to an extent, affect the entire system. Roger Harrison's four-culture typology, adapted by Charles Handy, suggests that unlike organizational culture, corporate culture can be 'imported'. For example, computer technicians will have expertise, language and behaviors gained independently of the organization, but their presence can influence the culture of the organization as a whole.

Strong culture is said to exist where staff respond to stimulus because of their alignment to organizational values. In such environments, strong cultures help firms operate like well-oiled machines, cruising along with outstanding execution and perhaps minor tweaking of existing procedures here and there. Conversely, there is weak culture where there is little alignment with organizational values and control must be exercised through extensive procedures and bureaucracy.

Where culture is strong—people do things because they believe it is the right thing to do—there is a risk of another phenomenon, Groupthink. "Groupthink" was described by Irving L. Janis. He defined it as "**...a quick and easy way to refer to a mode of thinking that people engage when they are deeply involved in a cohesive in group, when members' strivings for unanimity override their motivation to realistically appraise alternatives of action.**"

This is a state where people, even if they have different ideas, do not challenge organizational thinking, and therefore there is a reduced capacity for innovative thoughts. This could occur, for example, where there is heavy reliance on a central charismatic figure in the organization, or where there is an evangelical belief in the organization's values, or also in groups where a friendly climate is at the base of their identity (avoidance of conflict).

In fact group think is very common, it happens often, in almost every group. Members that are defiant are often turned down or seen as a negative influence by the rest of the group, because they bring conflict. Innovative organizations need individuals who are prepared to challenge the status quo—be it groupthink or bureaucracy, and also need procedures to implement new ideas effectively.

CHANGING THE CULTURE

Members of an organization often take its culture for granted and do not truly evaluate its impact on decisions, behavior, and communication, or consider the symbolic and structural boundaries of organizational culture until external forces test it. Therefore, when initiating transformation efforts it becomes critical to understand and explicate the values and personal meanings that define organizational culture.

In studies of organizational changes, researchers have found that organizations characterized by collegial values (i.e., teamwork, participation, commitment, and high levels of affiliation) looked at change enthusiastically and in positive terms as opposed to organizations characterized by gift edged or leadership-style value structures, which were more likely to view change negatively.

To bring about change, perform an organizational assessment.

The organizational assessment must include questions regarding the characteristics of institutional leadership, resource allocation, institutional structure, the flow of decision-making, and ties to external organizations. The assessment represents one of the primary steps to develop a cultural change. Next develop a culture of trust. While trust is most readily achieved through open communication between individuals and groups, trust is also enhanced when there is a history of making decisions together and with discussions of pros and cons.

Finally there is a need, for the use of planning strategies that are open, participative, aligned with the new culture and goals. Strategies characterized by these values also facilitate the development of trust, and can help develop institutional *"buy-in to the new way"*.

EXERCISE

Make an assessment of your staff. Identify which employees will be asked to be on the team.

Present the reason of why you have chose them.

RESISTANCE

Is the phenomenon often encountered when employees feel that they are losing control. This could be either directly or indirectly. The only way to fight resistance is by *reminiscence*, *duplication*, and ***working through the resistance***.

Reminisce to your staff of how things were and how far you have come. How the consistent drive to the change in culture will benefit the department.

Duplicate and repeat everything. People, by nature, are creatures of habit. When the habit is repeated it becomes the "norm" and before long they will be doing it because this is now the "norm". Work through the resistance, change is difficult; always reassure the employees that it's for the best. Take time to explain new procedures, do not implement then immediately, and give the employees at least five days to process the new procedures.

Chapter Two

BUILDING A TEAM

Shifting the way we do things.

Paradigm shift.

In the later part of the 1990s this emerged as a buzzword. The term was first used by Thomas Kuhn in his influential book *The Structure of Scientific Revolutions (1962)* to describe a change in basic assumptions within the ruling theory of science.

Today it has found uses in other contexts, representing the notion of a major change in a certain thought-pattern. — A radical change in personal beliefs, complex systems or organizations, replacing the former way of thinking or organizing in a radically different way. Most of our departments have been working with an autocratic style manager. He makes all the decisions, keeping the information and decision making among senior management. Objectives and tasks are set and the workforce is expected to do exactly as required.

The communication involved with this method is mainly downward, from the leader to the subordinate. This method can lead to a decrease in motivation from the employee's point of view. The main advantage of this style is that the direction of the business will remain constant, and the decisions will all be similar, which in turn can project an image of a confident, well managed business. On the other hand, subordinates may become highly dependent upon the leaders and supervision may be needed. This style worked for many years, but in today's ever changing and complex world it is really not productive. Chris Fest is the founder of a unique management style. The Laissez-faire style.

In a Laissez-Faire leadership style, the leader's role is peripheral and staff manage their own areas; the leader becomes a coach and ultimately make the final decision. However most of the supervision and control of a division's destiny is determined by a supervisor. The communication in this style is horizontal, meaning that it is equal in both directions, with little communication in comparison with other styles. The style brings out the best in highly professional and creative groups of employees. The process of agreeing upon objectives within an organization is extremely important.

Objectives need quantifying and monitoring. Reliable management information systems are needed to establish relevant objectives and monitor their "reach ratio" in an objective way. This requires a special person. To develop any system you must begin with a team.

The team must buy into the program and concepts of the program. Do not despair if the belief is really not there, it will come when the team sees the results. Whether it's on the playing field or in the workplace, teams take time to come together. There is a natural development process every team progresses through. It is useful to examine this maturation so that as a team member, leader, or facilitator you can be prepared to work effectively with the team.

REACHING OUT WITHIN

In the world of business a popular book by Jim Collins became an overnight success at the end of the century. The book, entitled "From Good to Great" documents the discovery of a research team, led by Collins, in the analytical survey of American corporations and how they went from just being plain good to great American icons.

The book became a household name in American corporate world and business academia.

I point this particular book, because is time that we start thinking as ourselves as "Business". While we do not provide a profit to our share holders, we do provide a service. We do have to answer to our constituents and taxpayers, justify our expenses and develop short and long term plans. While we are not a "Business", as the old saying goes, "Walks like a dog, wag the tail like a dog, bark like a dog then it must be a dog!"

We act like a business, operate like a business, our organizational structure is like a business, so why so many of us refuse to call ourselves a business I will never understand.

Back to aforementioned book. An interesting factor that the research of all of the companies that were identified as making the transition from good to great, one particular common denominator stood out.

All of the major corporations hired or used their own people to lead the corporation. One of the five factors identified in the research, amongst the successful companies was the component that they all hired their chief executive officer or chief executive from within the corporate structure.

No outsiders were there. Imagine a stock boy turned C.E. O. The theory is that the employees know what is better for the company, what works, what does not work and what they would like to change to make the work better. Better work means greater production. If you can afford to hire motivated employees, please do so. However, fiscal reality will most likely not allow employing anyone new. Within your organization there are enthusiastic, highly creative, and motivated employees. The culture of the department has kept them at bay. Now that you have changed style, this is time for you to seek them out and nurture them to reach their potential. Chances are that you already have an idea of who those employees are. During your honeymoon period at your new position or as a seasoned manager you have a pretty good idea of who is capable and who is not. However, your opinion may be biased. Put them to the performance test.

BUILDING YOUR GOAL

Practice insight to action theory. A good performance measurement program's main ingredient is making plans, taking action to collect information and data, subsequently turning that information and data into a higher performance. All of this while strengthening the relationship between management and the people who take the action to achieve higher performance.

You as a manager know in what direction you want to go. But you can't do it alone. You need a team of people to drive to the ultimate goal. On a sheet of paper outline the course to implement the goal. Try not to go into details; we will go there later in this chapter. Outline what you need in six phases. Now divide each of those phases into six additional sub-phases and so forth until you have simplified the master goal into different chapters, sub chapters and subdivisions each with an individual task. Itemize them and prioritize them in chronological order.

EXERCISE

As a manager, write objectives to the implementation of the program. What would you like to monitor and why. How you are going to monitor them and what good the data collected will do for the department.

Prepare a presentation.

PERFORMANCE EXPERIMENT

I learned this a long time ago. In order to find out the employee's potential do not assume anything. Some will shock you, others will disappoint you. People are not inclined to define their weak points. It is your duty, as a manager, to seek the best employee for the job to maximize productivity. Now that you have a road map, you need a vehicle. Call in to your office each potential team member. Discuss with him the subdivision and express enthusiasm and trust. Assign to him/her the task of getting it done. Agree on deadlines and the importance of the assignment. Give the employee the authority and power to make their conclusions and develop strategy to achieve the completion of the task. Tell the employee that this is their project and you won't interfere, however if they encounter resistance from other employees in obtaining data for the completion of the task, they should feel free to seek your advice. More importantly, assure that incompletion of the task will not result in any negative action. Always reinforce your trust and faith in him/her in getting the task completed. Let them go. Do not constantly ask how they are doing.

Resist the drain that the employee will impose on you. They seek you out to receive acceptance on what they are doing. They will approach you either officially or casually during the process and they will ask for your opinion, in essence your approval. Resist the strong temptation to jump in and take over, as you always did. Remember this is a test for you to find out what the potential of this employee is! When the project is completed, take the time to schedule a meeting with the employee and devote some quality time to exclusively hear how the conclusions were arrived at. Listen to how the process was carried out, including the creativity that was used to achieve the result. Take into consideration the enthusiasm and processing that the employee utilized when making his/her presentation. Is it sincere, is it passionate, and is the employee showing interest for more assignments?

Thank the employee for a job well done and be sincere about the completion of *their* project. Assure that their project completion will help the organization, no matter how trivial or minute the employee thinks it was. Let a couple of days pass before you review it again. Take some time alone, to review in detail the report or results from the assignment. Is it to your expectation, does it exceed the expectations? Is it valuable? Was it performed with pride and enthusiasm? Overall, is the employee competent to graduate to the next task? When selecting the next task, re-perform the aforementioned.

This time, and thereafter, the task is going to be a little more difficult and each time thereafter more complex and requiring more creativity, skills and dedication from the employee. Continue this process until all of your chapters are completed. By the way, I must emphasize that this method could be performed with different employees as long as different employees work on a different chapter. I am pretty sure that two things will happen.

Either the master goal will be ready to be implemented or the employee will reach a point that he/she cannot move from. This is their threshold. You have just learned the limits of this employee. He/she has just told you that they have reached their level of effectiveness. Now you know which of the employees has the strong features to add to the team. Select those employees who have the potential to bring a skill to the team.

The Team

A team comprises a group of people,
linked in a common purpose.

When putting people together, leave the micro management outside.

Teams work better independently and must be left alone to appropriately conduct tasks that are high in complexity and have many interdependent subtasks. ***A group in itself does not necessarily constitute a team.***

Teams normally have members with complementary skills and generate synergy through a coordinated effort which allows each member to maximize his or her strengths and minimize his or her weaknesses. Imagine a baseball team that assigned players to a different position everyday.

Consider working in a company where one day you're an accountant, the next day a security guard, another day, you're assigned as a salesperson. Chances are, with both the baseball team and company; success would not come easy, if at all!. Separate each of your department tasks and duties, select a team leader and allow the leaders to make their own decisions. He or she should work independently and be self managed. In today's industry a need for independence is a must. Many managers feel that direct input and *"Control"* of every single aspect of the department and its division is important. That worked in the past.

SET GROUND RULES

Ground rules help manage group dynamics and establish how the team will operate. Groups function most effectively when they have up-front agreements on how they will conduct themselves, how decisions will be made, and when and where the team will meet.

One way to establish ground rules is to ask team members what the team would look like if it were operating effectively and accomplishing all of its goals. The facilitator might ask people what the behavioral norms and conduct would be. The product of this dialogue could form the vision for the team. Today research shows us that independence gets people motivated. Your role as a manager should be more like a coach. *Coaching* is a method of directing, instructing, and training a person or group of people, with the aim to achieve some goal or develop specific skills. There are many ways to coach, types of coaching and methods to coaching.

Direction may include motivational speaking. Training may include seminars, workshops, and supervised practice. This is your first task that you have to achieve to determine which coaching methods will be beneficial to your organization. Once the team is assembled, and each branch of your department has a direct supervisor that reports to you, the FSNP methods become important.

FORMING –STORMING- FORMING- PERFORMING (FSNP)

The Forming – Storming – Norming – Performing model of team development was first proposed by Bruce Tuckman in 1965. He maintained that these phases are all necessary and inevitable in order for the team to grow, to face up to challenges, to tackle problems, to find solutions, to plan work, and to deliver results. This model has become the basis for subsequent models of group development and team dynamics and a management theory frequently used to describe the behavior of existing teams. In the first stages of team building, the forming of the team takes place.

Forming

Can you recall your first day at school as a child, or perhaps your first day on a new job?. Everyone is polite, overly cautious, and generally doesn't know what to expect. In the Forming stage, team members are getting to know one another and getting comfortable with one another. Members will naturally try to understand their own roles, the roles of the other team members and their role within the group. This is entirely natural and is to be expected. People are unsure, suspicious and nervous. The team meets and learns about the opportunities and challenges, then agrees on goals and begins to tackle the tasks. Team members tend to behave quite independently. They may be motivated but are usually relatively uninformed of the issues and objectives of the team. Team members are usually on their best behavior but very focused on themselves. Mature team members begin to model appropriate behavior even at this early phase. Sharing the knowledge of the concept of "**Teams - Forming, Storming, Norming, and Performing**" is extremely helpful to the team. Supervisors of the team tend to need to be directive during this phase. Help team members get to know one another. Make sure the purpose and task are clearly defined and share management expectations of the group. Give the team time to get comfortable with each other, but move the team along as well. The forming stage of any team is important because in this stage the members of the team get to know one another and make new friends. This is also a good opportunity to see how each member of the team works as an individual and how they respond to pressure. For our purposes, forming would consist of getting the team together to talk about the objective and why everyone on the team was selected. Emphasize the positive strengths that everyone will bring to the team.

STORMING

Once the team works together for a while, they will leave the forming stage and enter the storming stage. Politeness begins to evaporate and dissension occurs over basic mission and operating procedures. Control often becomes the primary issue. Who is going to make the decisions? Disagreements can be either very obvious or subtle. Storming is the most difficult stage for a team to endure, but it is necessary for healthy team development. When team members begin to trust one another enough to air differences, this signals the readiness to work things out. The team addresses issues such as what problems they are really supposed to solve, how they will function both independently and together and what leadership model they will accept. Team members open up to each other and confront each other's ideas and perspectives. In some cases *storming* can be resolved quickly. In others, the team never leaves this stage. The maturity of some team members usually determines whether the team will ever move out of this stage. Some team members will focus on minutiae to evade real issues. The storming stage is necessary to the growth of the team. It can be contentious, unpleasant and even painful to members of the team who are averse to conflict. Tolerance of each team member and their differences need to be emphasized. Without tolerance and patience the team will fail. This phase can become destructive to the team and will lower motivation if allowed to become disorganized. Supervisors of the team during this phase may be more accessible but tend to still need to be direct in their guidance of decision-making and professional behavior. Don't ignore the Storming stage. Acknowledge it with the team as a natural developmental step. Facilitators should acknowledge the conflicts and address them. This is a good time to review ground rules, revisit the purpose and related administrative issues of the team. This is the think tank of the team. What steps we need to take in order to accomplish our goals, should be a vocally presented. Disagreements are healthy. These team members were chosen for the ability to have a bird's eye view of the situation and may reveal to you, the manager, potential pitfalls that you may not be aware of. Do the department supervisors have the ability to achieve your ultimate goal?

NORMING

Team members adjust their behavior to each other as they develop work habits that make teamwork seem more natural and fluid. Team members often work through this stage by agreeing on rules, values, professional behavior, shared methods, working tools and even taboos. During this phase, team members begin to trust each other. Motivation increases as the team gets more acquainted with the project. Teams in this phase may lose their creativity if the norming behaviors become too strong and begin to stifle healthy dissent and the team begins to exhibit *groupthink*. You know you have reached the norming stage when team members begin to ask "How are we going to accomplish our assignment?" Beyond the politeness and nervousness of forming and beyond the issues and concerns of storming, teams will want to review how they are functioning. As team members learn to resolve their differences and emotional conflicts are reduced, they will have more time and energy to focus on their purpose. Supervisors of the team during this phase tend to be more involved than in the earlier stages. The team members can be expected to take more responsibility for making decisions and for their professional behavior. At this stage, the team has **process** down fairly well. *task* will take on new significance as the team will want to accomplish its purpose. You should keep this in mind and remind the team of the task. Also, you should be more diligent in adhering to the blue print, providing time for feedback, closure, etc. Initial impressions of members begin to change as they know each other better. The team feels a sense of achievement for advancement; however some begin to feel threatened by the amount of responsibility they have been given. They would try to resist the pressure and resist reverting to storming again.

Performing

The team has reached the final stage of development. Performing teams are just that, a highly effective, problem-solving unit that can reach solutions quickly and can even avoid issues before they become problems. These high-performing teams are now able to function as a unit as they find ways to get the assignment completed smoothly and effectively without inappropriate conflict or the need for external supervision. Team members have become interdependent. By this time they are motivated and knowledgeable. The team members are now competent, autonomous and able to handle the decision-making process without supervision. Dissension is expected and tolerated as long as it is channeled through means acceptable to the team. Supervisors of the team during this phase are almost always a participant. The team will make the majority of the necessary decisions. Teams at the performing level are generally self-regulating. Road maps, thought processes, decision making, and other concerns of team management will be handled independently by the team. Now that you have a team, Prioritizing is useful a useful tool in identifying what is important to the team.

PRIORITIZE

Prioritizing is simply voting on the items, ideas or actions facing the team. How those votes are cast or collected is important. A good rule of thumb is to allow each team member a number of votes equal to 1/4 of the total items on the list. For example, if the list numbers 12 ideas, each team member can vote for his or her top 3 selections. Here are some ideas for the process of prioritizing. Ask each team member to select his or her top choice from the collected list. Place a check mark next to the selection. Once everyone has indicated his or her first choice, continue the process for collecting subsequent choices.

Get-Up - Invite team members to come to the front of the room and indicate their own choices. It's good to get people moving about. Be sensitive to any requirements of people with disabilities. Group Like Items - If two suggestions are identical or similar, group together as one. Slip Method - If the topic is sensitive, use the slip method to prioritize. Direct the team to write down their selections, and collect responses. This avoids people having to publicly indicate their preferences. Generally, prioritizing is good for helping the team determine what it values, and it can be used to come to a decision or determine the team's preference. Prioritizing is useful whenever the team begins to feel stifled or unsure of what to do next. Prioritizing is a useful technique for cutting through clutter and identifying those items or issues critical to the team.

PARKING LOTS

Parking lots are temporary holding areas for ideas or suggestions that are not directly on-topic with the issue facing the group. It reminds the team member that his or her idea will not be discounted and could form the basis for a follow-up agenda or discussion point.

Introduce the concept of the parking lot early in the meeting. Keep a separate chart labeled "Parking Lot" visible in the front of the room. If an idea is submitted, and the team agrees it's worthy of discussion, but not at this time, place the idea in the parking lot for later discussion. At the conclusion of the meeting, review the parking lot items. Some may have been resolved during the normal course of the meeting. Others may not. Poll the group for those parking lot items that should be discussed at the next meeting.

An idea or suggestion that the team agrees merits additional discussion is brought up during the meeting. However, no one is quite sure how the suggestion "fits" or moves the process along. This is a good item for the parking lot. Once the idea is acknowledged and documented, move on. Address the parking lot issues later in the meeting or at a future meeting. Parking lots are visible reminders. Be sure to keep your group's parking lot visible to everyone. Parking lot items should be part of the meeting record.

Road Maps

A road map is an agenda format that organizes an effective meeting. It helps a team know and agree on what they want to address (the topic) and how (the process) they will proceed. Road maps offer an advantage over traditional bulleted agendas because road maps define *desired outcomes* and assign *time* limits to each step. The team leader is responsible for identifying the tasks and outcomes, and the facilitator selects the process. Road maps can be prepared prior to the meeting and confirmed when the meeting begins, or road maps can be developed at the onset of the meeting. Agenda items for the road map can be identified at the beginning of the meeting, which allows team input. While these options are available, it is preferable to have the roadmap completed by the facilitator and the meeting sponsor/convener but allowing the opportunity for additions by the team. Once the road map is agreed upon, the facilitator has the primary responsibility for ensuring that the data collected is accurate and aides the achievement of the goal.

Chapter Three

TASKS

Tasks are part of a set of actions
which accomplish a job.

Now that you have a team you have to get to work. What is this energetic, well tuned team to do? Assign each member of your team a task. One member can design the form, another can interview the division's supervisors to determine which data should be monitored, and another can assist with computer data collecting. The non negotiable items for the groups are as follows:

1. The data will be collected daily.

Everyday! For the program to be successful, data collection must be consistent.

2. Bi-weekly cycle reporting.

The data collected will generate a report within a 14 day period. This is manageable and more importantly, as we will discuss later in the chapter, it is a reasonable time for corrective action to be taken.

3. The day, location and time of the report are fixed.

No matter what the day, location and time that the group selects, that will be the day, time and location that regardless of vacation, weather conditions or any other reasonable or unreasonable events may occur.

If you recall from a previous chapter, set rules, guidelines, and deadlines "The only way to fight resistance is by reminiscence, *duplication*, and working through the resistance." I recommend meeting with the team on a weekly basis. This day of the week will set the tone for what day of the week your Citistat meeting will be set. The second item that you must report on and monitor are absenteeism, and overtime. Create categories for each employee.

You need this data to demonstrate distinctive patterns and track overtime expenses throughout a 14 day period. This information will be useful in developing you cost cutting practices that you can be adopted for each individual division. At your next meeting, after reviewing how the collection of data is preceding set a *"Live"* day. This day will be the day that the program will become active, instituted and set. Allow members of the team to discuss in detail their data collection. Monitor the progress. Their initial list will have an enormous listing of tasks. You as managers will have the choice of what will be important for you to monitor. Attempt to merge the listing into categories. Do this with every division. Remember that the listing should be manageable; I always say "Try to fit the round peg into the square hole". The list should merge two or three tasks into one. You do not want to overwhelm the employees with a never ending list of every single task that could be assigned.

The breakdown will give you the appropriate data of how many basins were inspected and how many of those inspected needed a follow up repair or cleaning. Do this with every division. Remember that the listing should be manageable; I always say "try to fit the round peg into the square hole". Once everyone agrees with what categories will be listed, have a meeting with that division supervisor, have him discuss with the team what is manageable and what other category he/she may want to add.

Empowering the supervisor will stimulate participation into the program.

SAMPLE CATEGORIES FOR PUBLIC WORKS DIVISIONS' COLLECTION DATA.

Personnell Data	Fleet Performance
Employee Leave	Fuel Usage
Task Performance	Disciplinary Actions
Permit Inspections	Citizens Request

EXERCISE

Present tasks that you will be monitoring and why.

FORM DESIGN

Now that you have identified each division task to monitor, the team must select and standardize the department's form. There are a few basic concepts of the forms. Compstat, Citistat and other performance based programs are not complicated. It simply allows you, the manager to run your department more efficiently. The technology fueling it is derived from off-the-shelf software, costing very little.

Like other data base programs you can, if you can afford it, hire a private consultant, purchase data base software or you can just use the software that is in your computer.

To begin I suggest to start with a minimum monetary outlay. There will be a 6 to 18 month curve for your divisions to get adjusted and tweak the problems that may arise. Investing a large amount of money may not be prudent. In total, Baltimore's CitiStat cost the city only $285,000 to set up, which included four full-time staffers, renovations to the new CitiStat Room in City Hall, and the software. In fiscal year 2001, the impact that CitiStat had on Baltimore's budget was an estimated savings of over $13 million, mostly the result of reduced operational costs, increased revenue streams, reduced absenteeism and job injury time utilization, and terminated costly and inconsistent initiatives. In my own town, the Citistat system began in 2006, and it cost the municipality $3,400.00 to set up. Again we use off the shelf software. In fiscal year 2007, the department of Public Works alone saved the taxpayers over $456,000.00 through the system. Since the reporting will be presented on a bi-weekly basis and the daily data forms will be compiled on a daily basis, all forms should look the same, for all the divisions. This re-enforces "Duplication".

I strongly suggest including day of the week and weather on all daily forms. The day of the week is important when evaluating data from the report because it becomes a tool to determine patterns. The weather is important because it can be another tool to explain low productivity in a particular task. Let's face it; you cannot fill as many pot holes when it's raining as opposed to when the weather conditions are favorable.

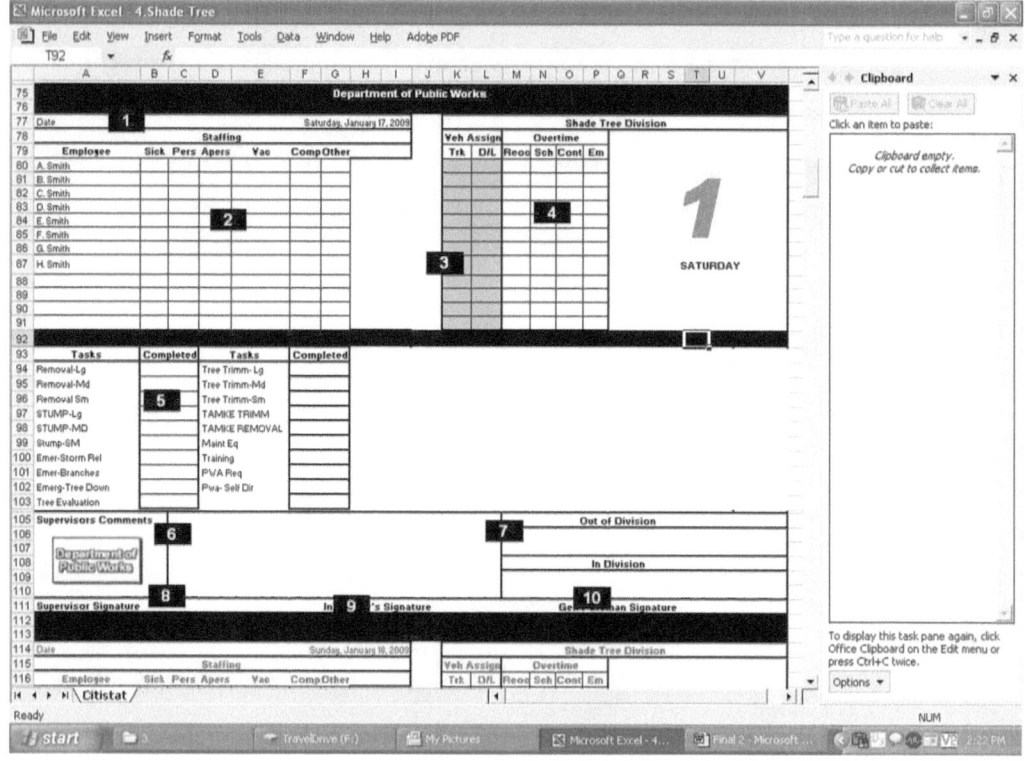

Fig 1 Sample Daily Report Form

1. Today's date
2. Staffing attendance
3. Vehicle assigned to staff
4. Overtime hours by each staff member
5. Tasks completed
6. Division's Supervisor comments
7. Supplemental staffing give to outside division
   Supplemental staffing received by this division
8. Supervisor signature
9. Superintendent signature
10. Other department leader signature (If necessary)

NOTES:

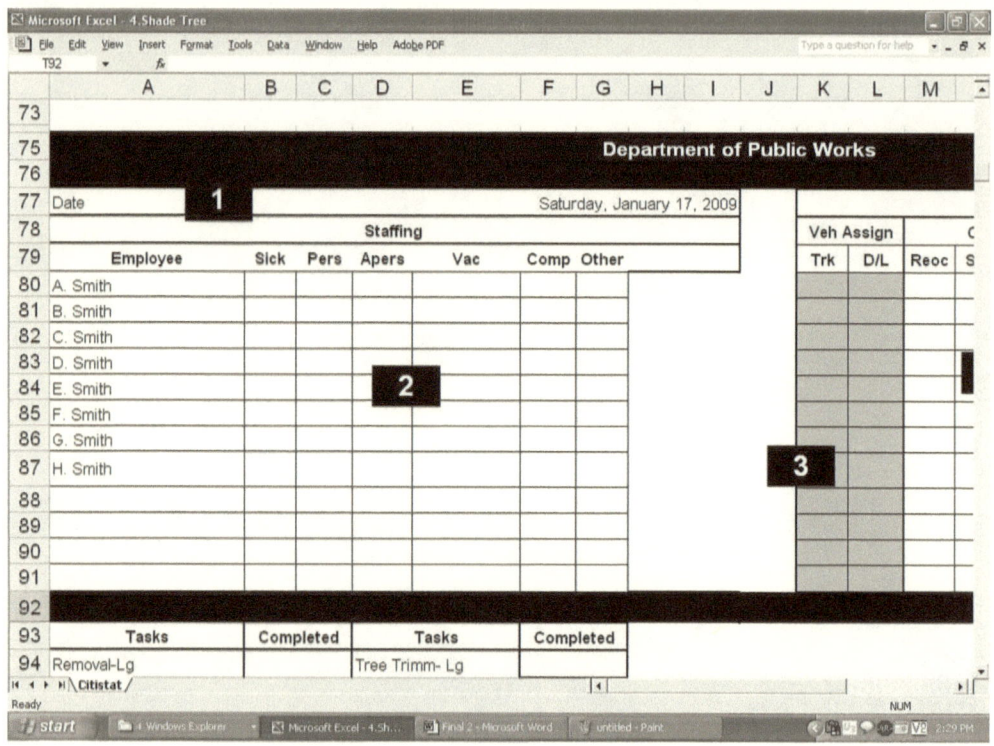

Fig 2. Attendance Section of Form
Detailed

1. Today's date
2. Staffing absences taken "Sick, Personal, Vacation, Compensatory, or Other"
3. Today's Vehicle assignment to staff member

ABSENCES AND ATTENDANCE

The daily report form should include attendance. Many departments have implemented absence policies which make no distinction between absences for genuine illness and absence for inappropriate reasons.

To defend abuse in absenteeism the department must take the total number and frequency of absences into account. Absenteeism reduces productivity among workers, and costs money. Departments often do excuse absenteeism caused by medical reasons if the worker supplies a doctor's note or other form of documentation. Sometimes, people choose not to show up for work and do not call in advance, which businesses may find to be unprofessional and inconsiderate. This is called a no call, no show.

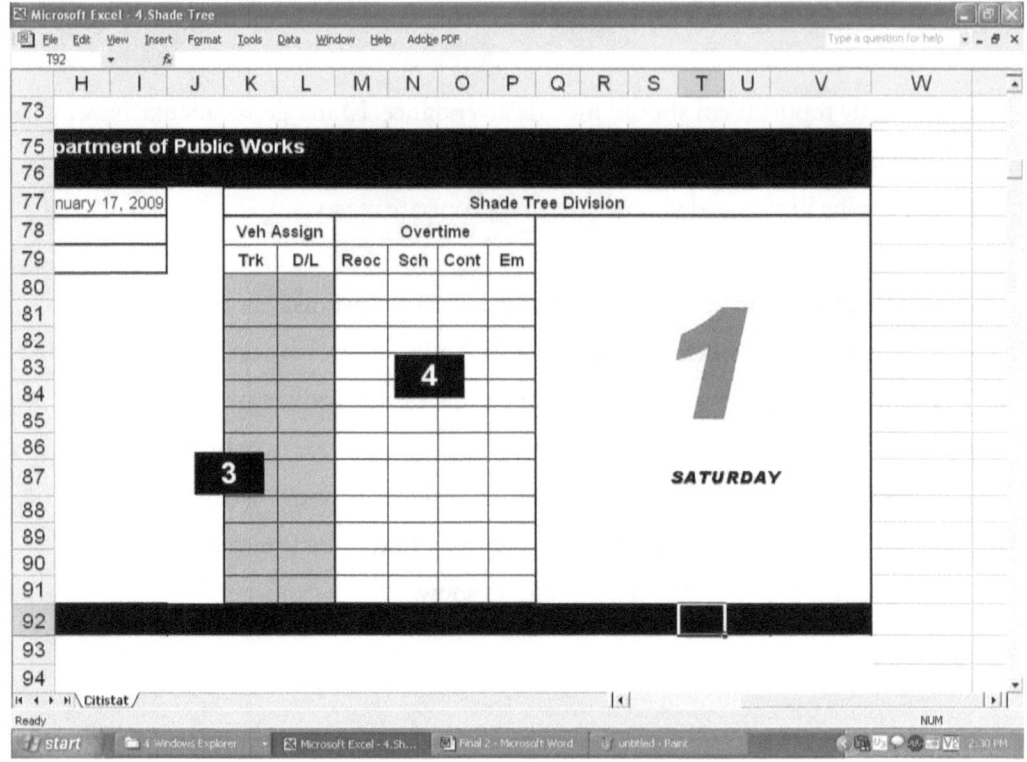

Fig 3 Sample Overtime/ Vehicle Assignement Section of Form
Detailed

3. Today's vehicle assignment to staff

4. Overtime incurred by employee defined as "Reoccurring,
   Scheduled,Continuation of day or Emergency"

OVERTIME/VEHICLE ASSIGNMENT

Overtime is the amount of time someone works beyond normal working hours. Normal hours may be determined in several ways: by custom, by practice, by legislation, or by agreement between employers and workers or their representatives. Most departments have overtime policies Overtime pay rates vary from department to department and can cause manager heartaches. Controlling overtime is a good indication that a manager is doing his/her job. Elected officials look at overtime expenditure as a waste of money. Overtime may be necessary, in emergency cases, but when overtime is *"calculated"* by the employee as part of salary it is an indication of inefficient management practices. If you want to score points immediately with the administrator(s), overtime reduction the best method of success.

This system allows you to look at patterns of overtime, when it occurs, and if as a manager you see a consistent pattern. It is your responsibility to review it and reduce it either through negotiation with the labor union or better deploying your resources.

You have just completed the "Human Resources" section of each division. Traditionally administrative personnel

Functions with performance were performed by one person in the office. Now you have empowered your supervisors to make the essential mid level management decision they can appreciate and direct resource planning at their level.

The objective of this system is to maximize the return on investment from the organization's human capital and minimize financial risk at the *"Trench"* level, so you as a manager would dedicate your time to bigger and better causes and minimally interfere with the day to day operations of the department.

EXERCISE

Discuss and present other possible monitoring human resources task that can be monitored and why?

NOTES:

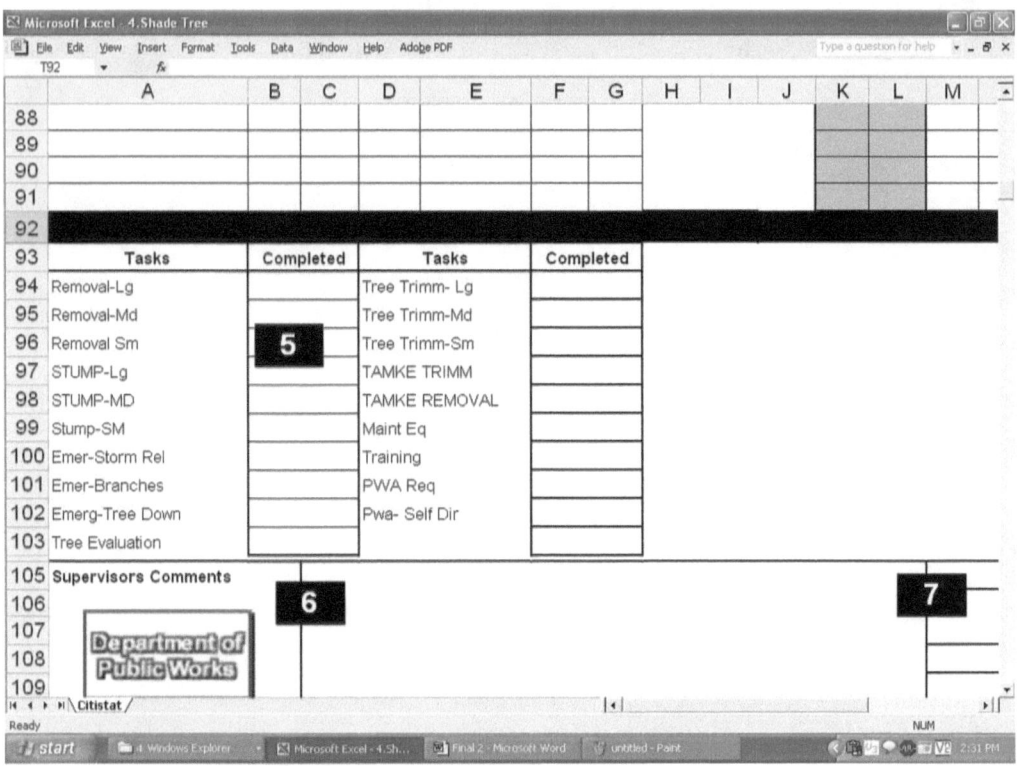

Fig 4 Task Section of Daily Form
Detailed

5. Today's numeric value of how many of each identified tasks were completed.

6. Supervisor additional comments that may not be included in the tasks activities.

TASK ASSESSMENT

Again, a task is part of a set of actions for each department division, which accomplish a job. A task is a synonym for activity although the latter carries the connotation of being possibly longer in duration. As I discussed in earlier chapters, assure that the task listed in the daily report is an activity that the division performs daily and you as a manager want to monitor. The activities noted, will be tracked from cycle to cycle, month to month , quarter to quarter and year to year to show progress or lack of thereof. I must emphasize, attempt to *"fit the round peg into the square hole"*. You cannot possibly monitor every single activity. You want to monitor the activities that are of concern to you. Although I stress counting the activities repetitively, tasks can be adjusted seasonally. As an example, the solid waste division may collect leaves during the fall season and grass in the spring season. The adjustment is really administrative rather than actual as the collection may be the same, but the disposal price may be different. These adjustments will happen from time to time, but I must stress, repetitiveness is a must whenever possible.

END OF DAILY REPORT

At the conclusion of the daily report you should allow the supervisor to enter comments on the day and his signature. With your signature you are affirming that the supervisor is actually accomplishing what he is documenting.

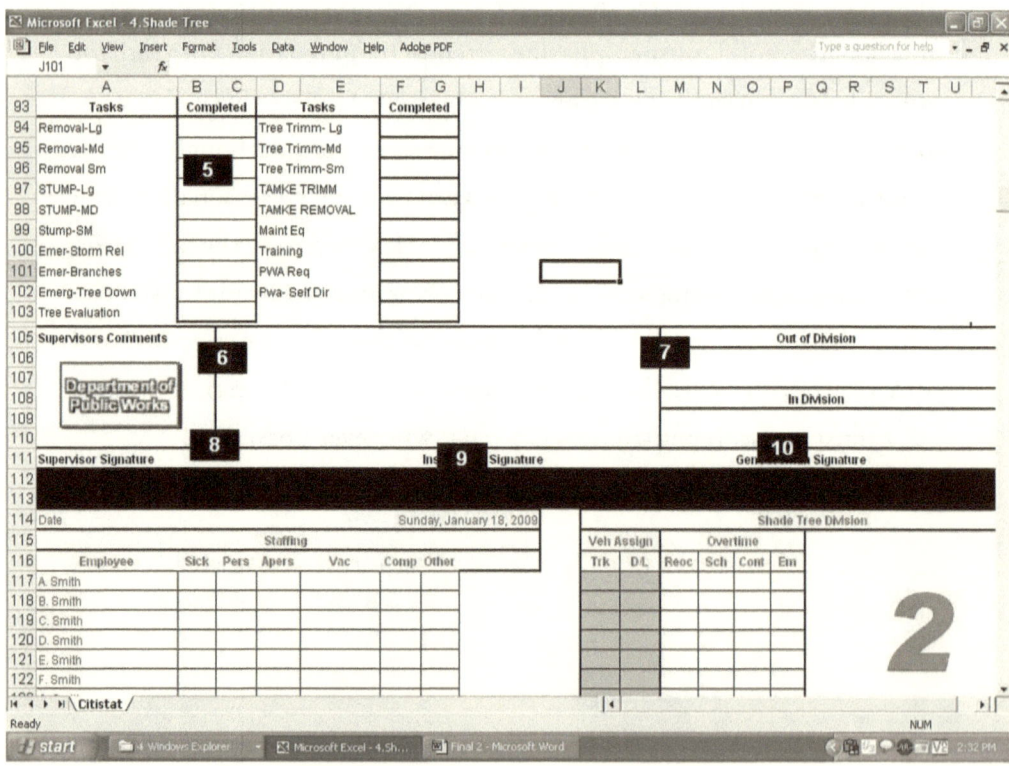

Fig 5 End of Daily Report Sections
Detailed

5. Today's numeric value of how many of each identified tasks were completed.

6. Supervisor additional comments that may not be included in the tasks activities.

7. Today's division staff that was assigned to another division
    Today's staff that was assigned from another division

8. Division Supervisor's confirming signature.

9. Department supervisor signature of review

10. (If necessary) Other department official's signature

Bring change
Slow....

People fear change.... Drive the change slowly!

egin with the team's original "Live Date" and a month before agreed date; make enough hard copies for all supervisors and divisions to use the daily sheets. Begin the process with hardcopies, no computers. This allows the employees to get used to the process and allows repetitiveness with the format. A month should give you enough time for a dress rehearsal (two 14 day cycles.) Cycle reporting should be at 00:00 Hrs (Midnight) of the beginning date until 23:59 Hrs of the ending date. As an example, if your cycle begins on a Monday, the reporting period should be on Sunday midnight (00:00) until the following Sunday at 11:59 P.M. Cycles become important when presentations are discussed.

Throughout this period you should be as patient as possible and the team should be available to anyone that asks for help. Situational management should be conducted. Whenever a situation arises, the team should unconditionally support the division and the supervisor in making the report. Reinforcement and support are key at this point. This is the foundation of success in the program. The team should be already working on the "Live" format of the program.

The Reporting Cycle Summary

By this time the team should have entered the daily form data into a spreadsheet format. Spreadsheets are practical because of the potentials of chart insertions and graphs. Remember, the supervisor will have to accrue 14 days of data, so whatever off the shelf software you are using should be duplicated 14 times, one for each day of the reporting cycle. The additions should be an aggregate for the entire 14 days.

THE PERFORMANCE CYCLE

This performance management program is based on the plan-do-review-revise-re-do cycle:

+ Plan: Understand current performance; prioritize what needs to be done.

+ Identify Actions that need to be taken and plan to improve those actions.

+ Do: Ensure that the proper systems and processes are in place to support improvement.

+ Take action : Manage risk – and help your staff achieve better performance.

+ Review: Understand the impact of your actions, review performance.

(Constantly speak to your staff, during this process, speak to the employees involved. Speak to them about their experience of performance problems with your actions and ways to improve it)

+ Revise: Using the lessons learned from review to change your plans or what you do so that future action is more efficient, effective and appropriate.

+ Go back to plan and start the cycle all over again until the system is made comfortable for everyone.

The stages will look and feel different depending on where you are in an organization and the timescale you are looking at. On an informal level, managers may set tasks, observe performance and give helpful feedback from day to day.

The different levels in this cycle need to be integrated across various organizational levels – and with partners.

This is sometimes described as the golden thread. Good and improving authorities usually describe their framework in a way that gives a clear picture of how different elements – for example, community planning, corporate policy, service and financial planning – fit together in the form of a long- or medium-term cycle.

SAMPLE DETAILED CYCLE																		
1.Date	4/1	4/2	4/3	4/4	4/5	4/6	4/8	4/9	4/10	4/11	4/12	4/13	4/15	4/16	TOT	Ave	Prev Cycle	Diff	YTD
2.Day of Week	Sat	Sun	Mon	Tue	Wed	Thu	Fri	Sat	Sun	Mon	Tue	Wed	Thu	Fri					
3.Weather	C	C	C	C	C	R	C	C	C	C	C	R	R	C					
4.Pot Holes			15	8	25	0	8				6	12	14	12	9	109	10.9	145	-36	4578
5.Patching			2	1	4	3	2				2	1	0	0	0	15	1.5	10	5	35
6.Resurfacing			0	0	0	1	0				0	0	0	0	1	2	0.2	7	-5	14
7. I 5 Used			30	45	15	60	19				25	35	7	12	75	323	32.3	257	66	789
8. I 2 Used			60	25	5	5	5				0	5	0	0	0	105	10.5	82	23	325
9. Sw. In Serv			2	2	2	4	4				4	4	4	4	4	34	3.4	34	0	68
10. # of St. Sw			230	230	230	357	308				307	308	257	402	402	3031	303.1	3015	16	6897

Fig 6- Sample of Cycle Report
Detailed

Type	Description	Reason
1. Date:	Report individual date.	Productivity by division broken into days
2. Day Of Week:	Report Individual date.	Day of week, Holidays, Overtime calculation
3. Weather:	Clear, Rain or Snow	May explain low productivity/ Reassignments.
4. Pot Holes:	Individual pot holes filled	**Total** indicates how many were filled in a cycle, **Average** per day, **Difference** will show productivity compared to previous cycle, **Year To Date** will indicate how may pot holes were filled for the year.
5. Patching	How many patches were	**Total** indicates how many were done in a cycle, **Average** completed per day per day, **Difference** will show productivity compared to previous cycle, **Year To Date** will indicate how many were done up to this cycle within the year.
6. Resurfacing	How many streets were	**Total** indicates how many were done in a cycle, **Average** resurface each cycle day. per day, **Difference** will show productivity compared to previous cycle, **Year To Date** will indicate how may pot holes were filled for the year.
7. I-5 Used	Material used daily	May explain how big the tasks were, Accounting.
8. I-2 Used	Material Used Daily	May explain how big the tasks were, Accounting.
9. Sweepers in Service	Daily Report	Equipment use, necessity for upgrade, staffing.
10. # of Streets swept	Daily Report	Services to residents, Average of how many streets are swept daily, Total of streets swept within the year SWPP Compliance.

Additionally, the team should design the presentation form to calculate an average for the entire cycle, a comparison to the previous cycle and a year to date aggregate. This can easily be accomplished by formulating the cells to calculate the average, difference from the previous cycle and this cycle, and the year to date linking the column to an accrued total.

THE TOTAL COLUMN

This column will add all of the daily data into one.

THE AVERAGE COLUMN

This gives the average of the task performed for the cycle. Averages can fluctuate depending on the frequency of activity. The average is the "Expected performance" for the division. Any fluctuation into a lower amount is indicative of loss of productivity.

THE PREVIOUS CYCLE COLUMN

This column compares the total of the current cycle to the previous one. A negative total is indicative that in the previous cycle a higher performance number was reported. A positive number is indicative that in this current cycle the division performed more activities when compared to the past cycle.

YEAR TO DATE COLUMN

This column is an aggregate of all tasks performed in this category for the entire program year. This information becomes extremely useful when compiling a yearly report.

EXERCISE

Discuss and present what you have as an idea where to hold these meetings. If there is not a room available, what other possibilities does your department have?

NOTES:

Chapter Four

GOING LIVE

Making the program work

Before going live with the program, make sure your staff is quasi-comfortable with the program's hardware. Don't put yourself into the "we need more time" mode as there will never be enough time. People normally resist change. Fourteen days before the beginning of the "Live Presentation' circulate a memorandum specifically outlining what the supervisor is expected to present. In the memo include that the presentation will be performed on the same day of the week, every two weeks. Explain how a two week cycle is a manageable time frame to take action and corrective measures.

Summarize the time frame that will be reported. Like many payrolls, the program will be reporting on the two previous weeks, not current events. This allows the supervisors to take corrective measure and allows for the corrective measures to be changed by the next presentation. Give a rough idea of whom, if anyone will be in attendance at the meeting. If elected officials or the Business administrator will be in attendance. Specify guest policies. More importantly is to be specific about the purpose of the program not being punitive, but corrective. Finally, be specific on what room and time (punctual) the meeting will be held, the uniform or dress code for the meeting, as these are all part of making the presentation "Official". Do not allow for "Absences". Have all supervisors designate alternates to deliver their presentation.

The Room

Designate a room where this event will be held. There are a number of thoughts on this issue. The first is taking the program reporting to an "Official" site, such as town hall or council chambers. The other is within the department's complex. Whatever your situation may be, do not choose a vagrant or roaming location. Clear the designated room for the day, in advance and attempt to be consistent!

The room should be practical, you as the manager should be seated at the "Head" of the table with all of the supervisors around you. The presentation podium should be located directly in front of you. The supervisor will be presenting the report to you, the manager, and all of the remaining supervisors should be on the sides accessible to view the presentation, make comments and suggestions.

THE SPEAKER

The speaker is the supervisor of the division that is making the presentation. He should stand up at the podium and make his/her presentation. Cycle dates, Attendance, overtime and tasks will be presented by all. The supervisor may choose to show a picture and bring to the floor any topic that pertains to his division at this time. He/she may also choose to open for discussion an incident or a situation that other division's supervisors may be able to assist in. This is a perfect opportunity for the supervisor to show and tell what his/her division did. Accolades, to particular employees who may have performed above average, should be acknowledged by the supervisor and manager. Every division will do the same.

THE MANAGER

After the supervisor has completed his presentation, you as the manager may question the supervisor on his or her division. Questions should be asked about attendance, equipment, performance, and patterns. If a problem is discovered, what step will the manager take to make corrections? This is a cordial and reciprocal exchange of thoughts, ideas and accountability. Any item that is unresolved will be placed on the "Re-Cap" list for the next meeting. Detailed maps and charts provide support for the numbers being reviewed. The manager should always reinforce the program tenets, as they are the main force and basis behind the program success that drives the entire department to the achievement of goals.

THE TENETS

Tenets are a doctrine held true. The Citistat or Compstat tenets foster a culture of accountability and resolution. The follow-up processes, and continual review of issues, will track particular problems and make their priorities clear to all. All meetings should start punctually and with a review of the tenets:

Accurate and Timely Intelligence Shared by All

Rapid Re-Deployment of Resources

Effective Tactics and Strategies

Relentless Follow-up and Assessment

ACCURATE AND TIMELY INTELLIGENCE SHARED BY ALL

Division supervisors are required to report on critical service initiatives and performance at bi-weekly meetings. All present must look for opportunities to improve coordination between divisions and identify strategies to improve departmental performance. Data should be accurate and specific. This is not the time you want to use percentages; you want to use exact and specific data to draw a clear picture of a problem. A problem is not a division challenge; it's a department problem, requiring departmental solution. Everyone's input should be considered. Our old style of doing things, isolating our division, is just not acceptable anymore. Ownership is shared. All supervisors share the success and failure of the department and therefore should share the solution to a challenge.

RAPID RE-DEPLOYMENT OF RESOURCES

Supervisors are required to re-deploy their resources to be more effective and efficient. All present will be part of the solution. A duck, is a duck, is a duck! Imagine a patrolman hearing that a traffic stop is within a block of his walking post. Does the patrolman say "I am the walking post and therefore I have nothing to do with that "or does he walk over to assist his fellow police officer? Employee assignments based on a Table of Organization need to operate the department. Our old method of performing tasks is too compartmentalized, unproductive, inefficient and ineffective to the overall operations of the department. If a division needs a truck, personnel, equipment and resources it's everyone's responsibility to make it work. A temporary assignment of personnel does not violate the labor collective bargaining agreement unless the employee is working outside the scope of his/her title. If a division can spare a man, truck or piece of equipment it is their duty to share that. Let's tear down the imaginary wall and boundaries that we have created and work together as one unit. Not only will the department benefit, supervisors will share and grow with the times.

EFFECTIVE TACTICS AND STRATEGIES

Each division's supervisors know what will work. They are empowered with applying effective strategies to bring resolutions to a problem. Often, our industry fails to use the available resources that we have. We take these for granted. This instance reminds me of a quote from Tip O'Neil's biography. Tip O'Neil was a seasoned statesman in the House of Representatives in Washington for decades before his retirement in the late 80's. In his biography he confided that, early in his career he lost an election back in his state of Massachusetts. When he returned to his district, as a losing congressional representative, he shared his loss with a constituent of his during a luncheon. To his surprise, the resident of his district confined in him that she had not voted for him, and she regretted it. Astonished, the seasoned politician could not make any sense of why the resident did not vote for him. After all, he thought, she was the right age, right political affiliation and textbook demographic to be his staunch supporter! He had to ask. He found the strength to ask the lady of why she did not vote for him. To his surprise, she replied "You did not ask me".

From this story, we learn a valuable lesson. We have personnel in our pool that has been in our department for years, they have seen it all; they have done it all and participated in practices that failed and worked. Ask them! See what worked in the past, and what did not. Most importantly; why it did not work. There may be an adjustment that can be made to make it work. Use your team, FSNP process to make the changes.

Relentless Follow-up and Assessment

Through the office of the department manager and the re-cap method, follow up is achieved, letting nothing fall trough the cracks. Self assessment of how we can do things better and more efficiently is presented at every meeting. Assign a person to specifically report the progress of the corrective measures taken. Have the supervisors lead the charge in discovering and taking corrective measures. The method that can be taken to justify inaction should not be assumed but explained by the supervisor. Let them take ownership of their malfunction or their accomplishment. Continuous follow-up is a must to achieve a productive action. Assessment must be monitored since the goal of the program is to move ever upward and reinvent our effective practices and distance our failing procedures.

EXERCISE

Discuss and present what more practices can the department take to meet the last two tenets of the program .How can it be done and how.

EXERCISE

Write the possible questions, you as a manager would ask your supervisors and why? Discuss other possible questions you can ask as a manager.

Mapping

Creating a Picture with Accurate Data

Whenever mapping is mentioned, people think of an unaffordable costs and walk away. The reality is that in today new technology, mapping is affordable and very easy to apply to existing software.

Your IT consultant or department would agree with me. There are a number of off the shelf programs that are very reasonable and easy to install. Additionally there are on line services that can be purchased through a contract that take the pressure of maintenance and compatibility away from your organization. Shop around; seek prices, logistical problem resolving protocols and compatibility with your current software. You will be surprise how affordable mapping has become.

This program, from its birth, relied on mapping to identify cluster of crime and trends. Because of the tactics used to control criminal activity, a computer generated history of the mapping, from the program inception to today, you can actually visualize the movement of criminal activity from an area to another.

While in Public Works we are not looking to move crime, we can utilize mapping to our advantage in a number of ways. Remember this entire program is designed to fit your individual organization's needs, you may deem that mapping may not be necessary, you may disagree to the type of mapping that other program have, however you do it, keep on asking the quantitative to qualitative question – what is that we want our quantitative data collected tell us, that we can turn into qualitative data!.

This approach in data mapping involves simultaneously evaluating actual data values in two data sources to point out peeks and deficiencies within a task. Statistics and percentages can be used to automatically discover complex opposing results between two data sets. This approach also allows you , the manager , to discovers data exceptions that do not follow the expected logic.

Here are some Public Works divisions' samples mapping strategies:

ROAD DIVISION

Quantitative Data =Pot Hole Mapping Chart
Qualitative Data=Areas of most pot holes
Result: Resurfacing Capital Project in that district.

GROUNDS DIVISION

Quantitative Data =Park Graffiti Events
Qualitative Data=Parks w/ high incidents of graffiti
Results: Share data with police to apprehend vandals, Increase lighting at night or placing of cameras in high frequency areas.

BUILDINGS & RECREATION

Quantitative Data = Park use by activity
Qualitative Data= Field use by activity/sport
Result: Field closure with rotation for full maintenance.

SHADE TREE DIVISION

Quantitative Data =Trees maintenance
Qualitative Data=Identification of Dangerous Trees *Results:* Plan to systematically remove dangerous trees from properties by district.

SEWER DIVISION

Quantitative Data =Sewer back up calls
Qualitative Data= Sewer line with high frequency of back up calls

MAPPING SAMPLE

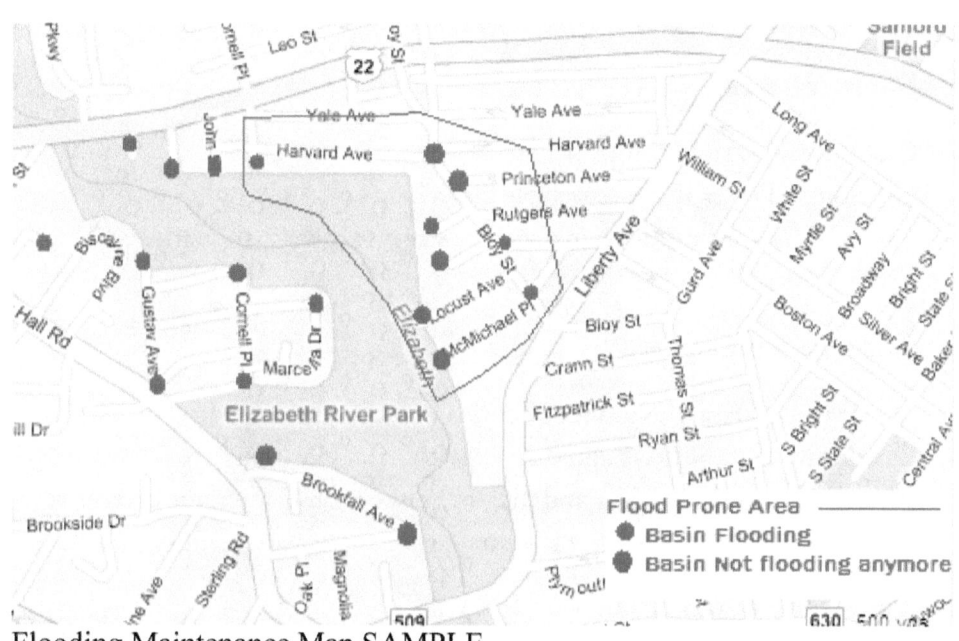

Flooding Maintenance Map SAMPLE

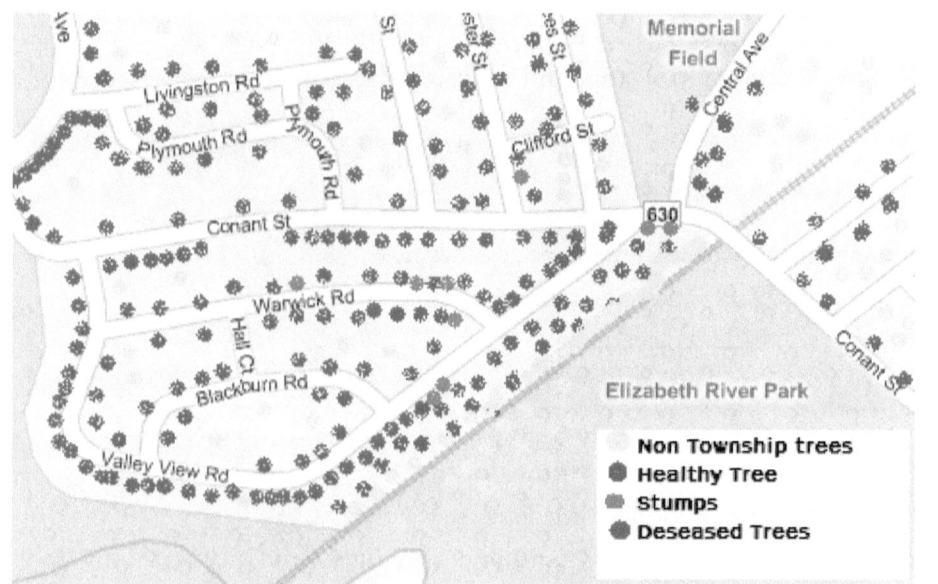

Shade Tree Map SAMPLE

Results: Weekly treatment of line, Line inspection for repairs, coordinate with health department for business inspection that may contribute to line obstruction (Grease, etc)

Solid Waste

Quantitative Date = Stops per route
Qualitative Data= Non recyclable households
Results: Educating residents in a specific street or district about the benefits of recycling

Code Enforcement

Quantitative Data = Number of notice of violations issued
Qualitative Data = Days and district with most violations
Results: educational project and increase inspection in areas for corrective measures.

Transportation

Quantitative Data = Shuttle stops
Qualitative Data = Stops with high and lowest users
Results= Combining of stops and addition of stop in other areas to better serve the residents.

Mechanics

Quantitative Data = Repairs made on vehicle
Qualitative Data = Specific vehicle repair
Results = Vehicle replacement

Finance

Quantitative Data = Expenditure
Qualitative Data = Budget line item expenditures
Results= Better financial handling of budget and accurate future appropriations. Multiple databases into a single stream data base identifying redundant purchases and expenses for consolidation or elimination.

Monthly Report

Preparing a monthly report

Preparing a monthly report can be useful to present to the Business Administrator, The Elected officials when seeking appropriations or explaining the impact of a budgetary reduction.

Or just to have as a reference.

Monthly reports should be compiled, since each cycle is 14 days, by adding two cycles.

Microsoft Excel - DATA

File   Edit   View   Insert   Format   Tools   Data   Window   Help   Adobe PDF

J8 ▾ *fx*

	A	B	C	D	E	F	G
1	ROAD DIVISION	Jan	Feb	March	Total	Average	YTD
2	Pot Holes Filled	3090	2542	845	938	2471.7	7415
3	I-5 Top	201	35	25	8	89.7	269
4	Cold Patch	1	5	6	7	6.3	19
5	Cold Patch Bulk	81	6	2	30	39.7	119
6	Crack Filling	0	0	0	0	0.0	0
7	# Of St Filled	10	1	34	0	15.0	45
8	90 Lb Rolls Used	59	9	0	0	22.7	68
9	Saw Cutting						
10	Sites	4	61	22	2	29.7	89
11	Saw Cutting (HRS)	4	121	86	29	80.0	240
12	Back Hoe Sites	16	71	194	94	125.0	375
13	Back Hoe Hrs	0	3	140	72	71.7	215
14	Patching	0	0	0	0	0.0	0
15	# of Sites	27	75	191	44	112.3	337
16	i5 Top	15	137	363	134	216.3	649
17	i-2 Base	11	66	34	114	75.0	225
18	H 4 1/4 top	0	428	33	24	161.7	485
19	Sweepers						
20	Sweepers In Sv	68	149	227	127	190.3	571
21	# Of Street Swept	1106	1749	3397	1851	2701.0	8103
22	Sweeper Mainte (HRS)	103	127	250	174	218.0	654
23	Sw. Details	38	21	50	26	45.0	135
24	Sw. @ Center	0	0	76	61	45.7	137
25	PWA						
26	Requests Closed	148	285	128	82	214.3	643
27	Self Direct	2253	1945	868	562	1876.0	5678
28	Zipper	0	6	3	52	20.3	61

When formulating the average remember to calculate the sum of the
six cycles divided by 84 , since each cycle has only 14 days.

A six cycle sequence creates a quarter. This will become useful when comparing year to year, since you want to compare the same performance in the same calendar year.

Each cycle should be separated by divisions . Just as the reporting cycle, the monthly report must encompass, a total, an average and a year to date.

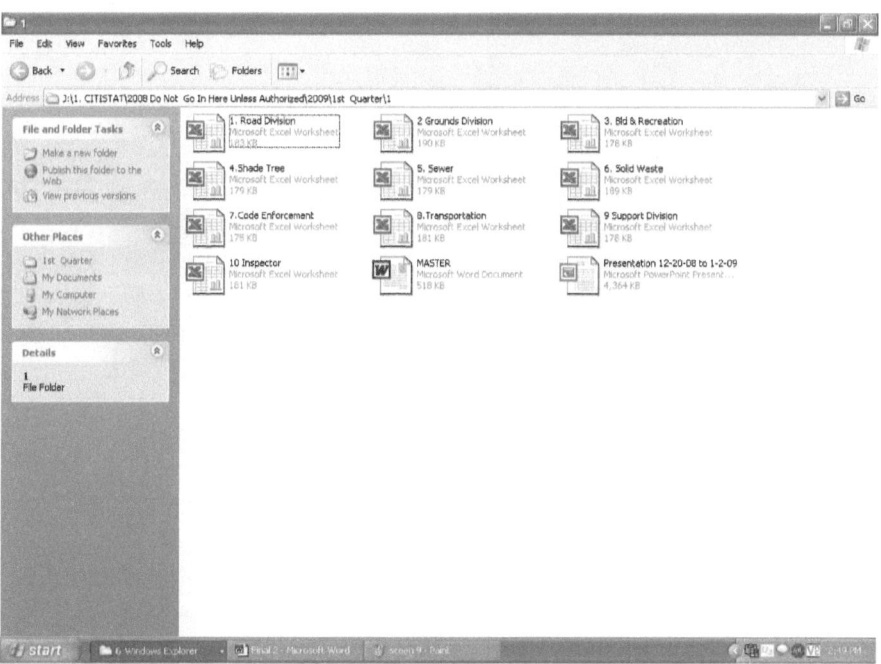

Formulating Quarters

A comparison from quarter to quarter will give the manager some insights on the department performance.

Quarterly reports not only are essentials to break down the year, but also are useful to compare cycle performance peaks and dips, for each divisions. Allowing the manager in making re-deployments of resources and personnel without negatively impacting on the overall performance of the department.

A suggested method is to divide the quarters into four, a trimester analysis of each division of the department

Quantitative and Qualitative

The entire objective for this program is to take "Quantitative" data a turning it into "Qualitative" data. Quantitative data is one that exists in a range of magnitudes, fields, and tasks and can therefore be measured. Measurements of any particular quantitative data are expressed as a specific quantity, referred to as a unit, multiplied by a number. Examples of quantitative data collection are pot holes, catch basin inspected, fields cuts, material used, and time.

The term of qualitative data is used to describe certain types of information. Qualitative data are described in terms of quality . This is the converse of quantitative, which more precisely describes data in terms of quantity and often using a numerical figure to represent something in a statement.

Quantitative data falls into two broad categories: Discrete (or attribute) data and Continuous (or variable) data. Discrete data generally falls into three categories: Category data (ie. car type), Bi-nominal data (ie. pass/fail), and Count / Poisson data (ie. # Of hairs on your head). Qualitative data are generally (but not always) of less value to scientific research than quantitative data, due to their subjective and intangible nature.

For our purpose, Quantitative is the "Mass numbers of data collected by the department" and Qualitative is the "The quality or specific of the data collected".

Here is a brief example:

The end of the year report shows that the Road Division filled 3480 Pot holes. The same report shows that the total costs for Pot Hole repair was $ 17,480.00. We can reasonably come to the conclusion that the average cost of each repair was $ 5.02. (17480/3480= 5.0229) without labor and equipment.

Now, your elected officials want to decrease the appropriation to the pot hole line item of the budget by 25%. The 25% decrease equals to $ 4370.00 (17480x .25= 4370). The new budget appropriation will be $13,110.

As public works manager is it your duty to advise them that there will be 871 (rounded off) less pot holes filled (4370/5.02)or 20% (rounded off) of decrease services to the residents, when compared to the previous year, if not more because you are assuming that the cost of the material will stay at the previous year's rate. These numbers are undisputable!

Same application can be done for all tasks that your department chooses to monitor and report. From Tree stumps, to street swept, all tasks can be transformed as a tool.

Here is another example:

As per your report, this cycle, 3 men swept 125 feet sidewalks. We can reasonably come to the conclusion that each man averaged 41.66 feet of sidewalk sweeping within this cycle (125/3= 41.66). The average man, in a ten day working cycle swept 4.16 feet of sidewalk per day. (41.66/10). This is a fact.

Management wants to reduce costs of operations and wants to reassign one of those men into a different position. As a manager you can argue with solid data that 42 feet of (rounded off) sidewalks will not be swept reducing services by 33% . No one can dispute these numbers.

The uniform services, Police and Fire Departments have been using this system for years, and the result are that there are far less Police and Fire services getting a budget reduction, when compared to their public works counterparts.

Problems with
This program

Every program has shortfalls, avoiding them is beneficial to the department's success of the program

Behn Robert, a lecturer from Harvard's Kennedy school of government has studied many "Performance based programs" like CitiStat and Compstat for many years.

I was privileged to be quoted on his blog earlier in 2006. Behn has identified seven crucial shortfalls with performance based programs.

1. Program with no real purpose

The program has no clear purpose of what is monitoring or what it is supposed to achieve. What is it that the implementation of this program is designed to do? Only you as a manager can determine that. Are the goals set clear for everyone to understand? Is everyone on the same Page" and although there may be some resistance, has it minimized throughout the implementation of the program.

2. No specific roles for participants

The program is in disarray of who is supposed to do what, collect what data and when. What is the role of the supervisor? How is the team of analysts interacting with each division supervisor? Have duties and responsibilities been clearly outlined? Is everyone capable of performing their job responsibility? In someone's absence who is the designated representative? Does he know what is expected of him or her?

3. Meetings held irregularly, randomly and infrequently, too informal

The program loses its values when there is no consistency. I must redirect you to the earlier chapters. Duplication! (Look back at "Resistance"). the most important aspect of the program is perception. As I am often quoted "Perception becomes reality!" If the program is constantly repeated it sends a message to the participant that the program is to be institutionalized and is here to stay. Effectiveness of the same day, same time each time is subliminal to the participants that may not be willing at first.

4. No one person is designated to run the meeting

Let's be honest, we as government workers suffers from the "Job Security" syndrome. It's a way that our industry and government in general, has operated for years. If Mary, whose responsibility is to make copies, is out, no one can make copies, because that's her job. As comical as that may sound, it's true. Well not everyone can run this meeting. A senior manager, a senior supervisor or equivalent, in the absence of the superintendent or director should be able to run the meeting. The exchange and dialogue of the presentation and the solution to the problems will exit once the meeting has started. Preferably choose a person that will conduct the meeting in the same professional manner as you, and notify those whom will be in attendance that the appointee will be conducting the meeting and he/she should be treated as an equal to you. You may have to take corrective measures with specific individuals that may not comply with your directive.

5. No dedicated analytical staff

You must establish an unbiased analytical staff for the data to be interpreted at its true value. The basis of this program is to analyze data and measure performance. A team should meet on a monthly basis to compare data from cycle to cycle, month to month, year to year. Most importantly the current cycle and a comparison to the previous year at the same time and cycle. His data will start to show patterns of personnel attendance shifts, performance and productivity. The tool given will help you make decisions in when to start that " Big" project where additional personnel is needed, or when to better accentuate your performance for a particular task.

6. Missing the follow up

Knowing that the issue is there and not following up on the progress of the correction will make the correction never happen. Things start going awry when provided services fall through the cracks. The resident's tree is not trimmed when promised; the street pot hole or flooding condition is not corrected. Follow-up is everyone's responsibility. The situation will get out of control if the leadership does not become relentless in the follow-up of issues, problems and tasks.

7. Meetings become brutal

These meeting are not supposed to be a "Roast". You can be critical of a practice, but when you become brutal it discourages people from coming forward. These meetings are to be productive not punitive. The entire program is designed to empower the line supervisor with the decision making. The attendees will become even more resistant if they feel that the meeting is designed to become a bash and roast of the supervisor. Use this meeting to ask about how his/her staff is doing, how the equipment is holding up. At many of our meetings we make sure we commend a particular employee that solved a problem in front of his peers. Have subordinate employees attend the meetings as guests so that they get to experience and see how their actions, or inactions, effect the division. Take the opportunity to reward the employees with perfect attendance or, a division that has reduced overtime. Everyone wants to be recognized and rewarded. This can be the perfect forum.

Conclusion

Regardless of what system you are using, you are ahead of everyone else.

I congratulate you for having the vision and the knowledge in establishing a system. The fact is that many public works agencies are not using any system. Although they may be collecting the data that this program needs to be started, they have no system in which to input it. The fact is that the uniformed divisions have been using this type of system to provide this data, to retain a structure of accountability and efficiency for quite some time. They are moving into the next level

Our industry has been working just as hard, perhaps harder; we just do not have any data for support. The uniformed divisions throughout their lobby have been effective in creating agencies within state and federal government to access and report the collected data. Our public works lobby is non existent and is more of a social and travel club for those who are officers of the organization. In essence, no interest has been given by local associations to establish a reporting system in a statewide format.

Our departments are in need of structure in such reporting formats. Like the Fire and Police, through the local government and office of the attorney general we eventually will be asked to interface and report our achievements, inspections, road sweeping, road repairs etc.

Some agencies are already asking for such raw data. It is up to all of us, you included, to bring the next generation to the forefront, so that during our next crisis we will have the necessary tools to repair the economy.

References used for this book

Cutting Crime and Restoring Order: What America Can Learn from New York's Finest by William J. Bratton

COMPSTAT Plus By George Gascón, Assistant Chief and Director of Operations, Los Angeles Police Department

The CitiStat Model: How Data-Driven Government Can Increase Efficiency and Effectiveness By Teresita Perez, Reece Rushing

Carlo M. Cipolla, Before the Industrial Revolution: European Society and Economy 1000-1700, W.W. Norton and Company, London (1980) ISBN 0-393-95115-4

Burnett White, Natural History of Infectious Diseases

Robert Youker, Changing Business Culture, World Bank

Charles W. L. Hill, and Gareth R. Jones, (2001) Strategic Management. Houghton Mifflin.

Robert Fulford, Globe and Mail (June 5, 1999).

'http://www.robertfulford.com/Paradigm.html' Retrieved on 2008-04-25.

www.hks.harvard.edu/thebehnreport/Behn,%207PerformanceStatErrors.pdf

Government are from Saturn, Citizens are from Jupiter, Strategies for reconnecting citizens, MRSC, Seattle Washington

Managerial Auditing Journal, ISSN: 0268-6902, Emerald Publishing Group

Performance Measurement and Metrics, ISSN: 1467-8047, Emerald Publishing Group

Benchmarking: An International Journal, ISSN 1463-5771, Emerald Publishing Group

Tuckman, Bruce. "Developmental sequence in small groups". *Psychological Bulletin* 63 (6): 384-99. Retrieved on 2008-11-10. "Reprinted with permission in Group Facilitation, Spring 2001".

Rickards, T., & Moger,S.T., (1999) Handbook for creative team leaders, Aldershot, Hants: Gower

Rickards, T., & Moger, S., (2000) 'Creative leadership processes in project team development: An alternative to Tuckman's stage model', British Journal of Management, Part 4, pp273-283

Knight, Pamela J., "Small, Short Duration Technical Team Dynamics", Defense Acquisition University Press, Fort Belvoir, VA (2006).

Collins, Jim. (2007) "Good to Great- Why some companies make the leap and others don't" Harper Collins,

PMMI from-Improvement and Development Agency Layden House 76-86 Turnmill Street London EC1M 5LG